Stephen C. Avery

Presented to:

Stephen C. Avery

by:

Mom & Dad

date:

Christmas 1992

◆ ◆ ◆

When things are hard to
understand, reading this will
help you to know why we
do what we do for you.

"More desirable than gold...
and sweeter than honey..."

That's what Psalm 19 says about Bible truths—
the same rich truths presented just for kids
in Questar's **Gold'n'Honey Books**

The Beginner's Bible

TIMELESS CHILDREN'S STORIES

as told by **KARYN HENLEY**
illustrated by **DENNAS DAVIS**

Questar Publishers, Inc., Post Office Box 1720, Sisters, Oregon 97759

Contents

Favorite Characters, Topics, & Stories
Where to Find Them in THE BEGINNER'S BIBLE

(Page numbers refer to the first page of each story)

TIMELESS STORIES
FROM THE OLD TESTAMENT

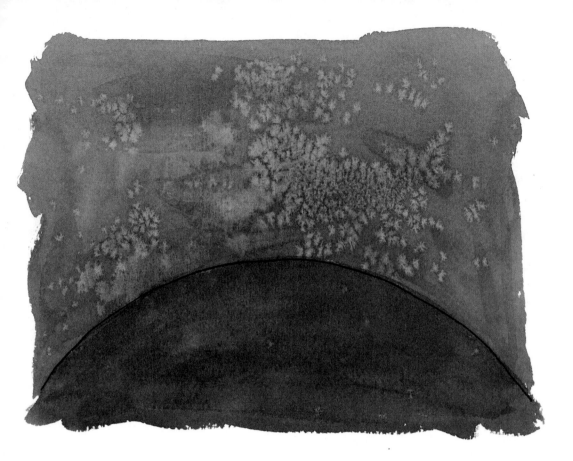

The Beginning

In the beginning, the earth was empty.
Darkness covered everything.
But God was there, and He had a plan.

CREATION, from Genesis 1

"Let there be light," He said.
And suddenly, golden light shone all around.
God called it "day."
He called the darkness "night."
With the light and the darkness,
the first day passed.

On the second day, God said,
"Let there be a great space."
So the space was formed, deep and high.
God called the space "sky."

God made rivers and seas on the third day.
He formed the mountains and deserts,
the islands and beaches.
He planted tall trees, swaying grasses,
and flowers of every color.

When the fourth day came,
God put lights in the sky:
the fiery sun for daytime,
the sparkling moon and dancing stars for night.

On the fifth day, God filled the water
with fishes of all shapes and sizes.
He made the birds to glide across the sky.

God made animals on the sixth day:
furry animals, scaly animals,
smooth, sleek animals.
And on that day, God made man.
When He was finished, God saw that
everything He had made was very good.
And on the seventh day He rested.

The Special Helper

Adam was the man that God made.
He had a very important job.
He gave names to all the animals.

ADAM & EVE, from Genesis 2

There were many wonderful animals.
But still, Adam was lonely.
God said, "It is not good
for Adam to be alone."
So God made . . .

a woman.
Adam named her Eve.
Eve was just right
to be Adam's special helper.

A Sad Day

Now Adam and Eve lived
in the beautiful garden of Eden.
Tasty fruit grew from many of its trees.
God told Adam and Eve
they could eat any fruit they wanted,
except one kind.
He said, "You must never eat the fruit
from the tree of the knowledge
of good and evil."

LEAVING THE GARDEN, from Genesis 3

One day, a snake came to Eve.
It said, "See how pretty the fruit is
on the tree of the knowledge of good and evil?
It tastes good.
It will make you wise.
Don't listen to God.
Go ahead and try it."

The fruit did look good.
So Eve ate some.
Then she took it to Adam.
He ate some, too,
even though he knew what God had said.

That evening, God walked through the garden.
Adam and Eve tried to hide.
God called, "Adam, where are you?"
Adam said, "I am hiding.
I was afraid."
Then God asked, "Did you eat the fruit
I told you not to eat?"

Adam said, "Eve ate it first."
Eve said, "The snake told me it would
be all right."
But God was not happy.

He told the snake, "You will have to crawl
on your belly from now on."
He told Adam and Eve,
"You did not obey me.
You will have to leave the garden."

It was a sad day when Adam and Eve left.
God sent an angel to the garden.
The angel held a flaming sword.
He flashed it back and forth
so no one would go back into the garden.

The First Rainbow

Many years passed after Adam and Eve
left the garden.
People began to forget about God.
They began to do bad things.
There was only one good man.
His name was Noah.

God said, "I am sorry that I made people.
I will start all over again."
God told Noah to build a big boat
called an "ark."
God showed Noah exactly how to build it.

When the ark was finished,
God told Noah to put animals in it.
Noah obeyed God.
He put some of every kind of animal
into the ark.
Then God shut the door.

Soon rain began to fall.
The raindrops made little puddles,
then bigger puddles.
The big puddles became streams,
then rushing rivers,
then sloshing seas.

Soon the whole earth was covered with water.
The ark tossed up and down on the waves.
But Noah and his family and all the animals
were safe and dry inside the ark.

Then one day the rain stopped.
Noah opened a window in the ark.
He saw water everywhere.
He sent a dove to fly out and look for land.
But the dove came right back.
It could not find a place to rest.
The next time Noah sent the dove,
it brought back an olive leaf.
The water was going down.
The next time, the dove did not come back.
It was time to leave the ark.

The ark was resting on top of a mountain.
Noah and his family and all the animals
came out.
Noah thanked God for keeping them safe.
Then God put a dazzling rainbow in the sky.
It was God's promise that water would never
again cover the whole earth.

A Tall Tower

When the world was new,
all people spoke the same language.
They had one word that meant "hello."
They had one word for "hungry,"
and one word for "tired."
They could talk to each other and
understand each other.

TOWER OF BABEL, from Genesis 11

One day while they were talking,
they got an idea.
They said, "Let's make some bricks
and build a tall tower.
Let's build it so tall that it reaches heaven.
Then everyone will say we are the
greatest people in the world."

But God did not want them to build
the tower.
He saw that they were selfish and proud.
So He gave each person a different language.
Now when one man spoke to another man,
all of his words sounded new and different.

The people were mixed up.
They could not understand each other.
They could not cooperate anymore.
So they stopped building their tower.
They called the unfinished tower "Babel,"
because God confused their language there.

A New Land

There once was a good man named Abraham.
God had a special plan for him.
God told Abraham to move to a new land.

ABRAHAM, from Genesis 12-17

So Abraham left the place where he lived.
He packed up everything he had:
his tents, his dishes, his clothes.
He gathered all his animals.
And he went to the new land
that God showed him.

Abraham's wife, Sarah, and his nephew, Lot,
went with him.
Abraham and Lot also brought along helpers
to take care of their animals.

But there was a problem:
Abraham's helpers and Lot's helpers
were always fighting.
Abraham said to Lot, "Let's not have
all this fighting.
You take your helpers and choose
a new place to live.
And I will take my helpers
and move to a different land."

Lot chose first.
He took the best looking land for himself.
It had plenty of water and grass
for his animals.

Abraham moved his animals and his family.
He set up his tents
near the big trees at Hebron.

God made a promise to Abraham.
He said, "You will have so many children
and grandchildren and great-grandchildren
that no one will be able to count them.
And all the land that you see right now
will be yours."

The Promise

Abraham was sitting by his tent
one very hot day.
He looked up and saw three men
standing nearby.
He was happy to have visitors.
He hurried to them and asked them
to stay for dinner.

BIRTH OF ISAAC, from Genesis 18 & 21

Then Abraham ran to his tent.
"Quick, Sarah," he said.
"Get some flour and bake some bread.
We are having guests for dinner."

Sarah made a good dinner for them.
While they were eating,
the men said a very surprising thing.
They said, "Next year you and Sarah
will have a baby boy."

Now this was surprising, because Abraham
and Sarah did not have any children.
And they were too old to have a baby.
Sarah was listening in the tent.
She heard what the men said.
And she laughed.
She did not believe them.

Then God said, "Why did Sarah laugh?
Is anything too hard for the Lord?"
And God kept his promise.
Even though Abraham and Sarah were old,
God gave them a baby boy.
They named him Isaac.

A Wife For Isaac

When Isaac was grown,
Abraham wanted him to get married.
Abraham called a servant.
Abraham said, "Go back
to the land we came from.
Get a wife for Isaac there."

The servant took ten camels.
He traveled a long way.
One evening he came to the town of Nahor.
He stopped by a well.
He asked God to help him.
He prayed, "When the girls come
to get water at the well, show me
the girl you want for Isaac.
Let her give me a drink, and then
let her give my camels a drink, too."

Down to the well came a girl,
carrying a water pot.
Her name was Rebekah.
The servant asked her for a drink.
She gave him a drink.
Then she said, "I'll give water
to your camels, too."

The servant thanked God.
He knew that this was the girl
God had chosen.
He gave her a ring and two bracelets.
That night, he asked Rebekah's father
if she could marry Isaac.
Her father said yes.

So the next day,
Rebekah went with Abraham's servant.
Isaac loved Rebekah.
Rebekah married Isaac.
And they had twin boys named Esau and Jacob.

The Blessing

Isaac grew to be an old man.
His eyes could not see anymore.
He called Esau.
"I want to give you a special blessing,
so you will be a leader," he said.
"Make me some of my favorite food.
Then come back and I will bless you."

ISAAC BLESSES JACOB, from Genesis 27

Rebekah heard what Isaac told Esau.
Now God had told Rebekah
that Jacob would be the leader.
So Rebekah wanted Jacob to have the blessing.
She made Isaac's favorite food.
She covered Jacob's arms with goat skins
so he would feel hairy like Esau.

Jacob pretended to be Esau.
He took the food to Isaac.
Isaac felt Jacob's hairy arms.
He thought Jacob was Esau,
and he blessed Jacob.

Jacob's Dream

Esau was very angry when he found out
that Isaac gave Jacob the blessing.
So Rebekah sent Jacob away for awhile.
Jacob walked and walked.
When it was night, he stopped to rest.
He put a stone under his head for a pillow.

65

While he was sleeping,
he had a beautiful dream.
In his dream, he saw a ladder
going from the earth into heaven.
Angels were going up and down the ladder.
God was standing at the top.
God said, "I am taking care of you.
I will be with you wherever you go."

When Jacob woke up, he said,
"Now I know that God is with me."
He took the stone he had slept on
and stood it up.
He called that place Bethel.
He left the stone there
to remind him of his dream.

A Big Family

Jacob traveled far away to his uncle's house.
He worked for his uncle, taking care of sheep.
While he was there, Jacob got married.
He had twelve sons.
Jacob's big family lived on his uncle's land
for many years.
But Jacob wanted to go back home.

JACOB RETURNS, from Genesis 29-33

One day, Jacob packed up all his animals
and his family and everything he had.
They traveled all the way back
to where Esau lived.

Now Jacob was afraid
that Esau might still be angry at him.
So he sent presents to Esau.
He sent servants who said,
"Please don't be angry anymore."

But Esau wasn't angry.

He ran to Jacob.

He hugged and kissed him.

He was happy to see his brother again.

The Dreamer

Jacob lived in the land of Canaan.
He had twelve sons.
Joseph was one of his sons.
Jacob loved Joseph
more than all his other children.

One day, Jacob gave Joseph a new coat.
It was a beautiful coat.
It had many colors.
But it made Joseph's brothers jealous.
They wished they could have new coats, too.
They were angry.

Joseph also had a special dream.

He told his brothers about it.

"We were gathering grain in my dream.

My grain stood up.

Your grain bowed down to mine."

Joseph had another dream.
He said, "The sun, the moon and eleven stars
bowed down to me."
His brothers did not like his dreams.
They were jealous.

They wanted to get rid of Joseph.
So they sold him to some traders
who were traveling to far away lands.
The traders took Joseph far away to Egypt.
But God was still watching over Joseph.

A Secret Message

Joseph had a hard time in Egypt.
Even though he was good,
Joseph was put in jail.
But God was with Joseph.
The jailor liked Joseph.
He let Joseph take care of
the other prisoners.
One of the prisoners was a butler.
Before he was in jail, his job was to bring
the king of Egypt something to drink.

JOSEPH & PHARAOH'S DREAMS, from Genesis 39-41

One night, the butler had a dream.
He dreamed he was taking a drink to the king.
The butler told Joseph his dream.
Joseph said, "That means you will soon
be out of jail.
You will get to do your job again."

The butler did get out of jail.
Joseph asked the butler to remember him.
He wanted the butler to help him
get out of jail, too.
But the butler forgot.

One night, the king had a dream.
He dreamed that seven fat, juicy ears of corn
were growing on one stalk.
Then seven thin ears of corn grew up.
They swallowed the fat, juicy corn.

The king had another dream.
He dreamed that there were seven fat cows.
But seven thin cows gobbled them up.
The dreams made the king worry.

He asked his wise men what the dreams meant.
But they did not know.
Then the butler remembered Joseph.
He told the king about Joseph.

The king sent for Joseph.
Joseph told him, "Your dreams mean
Egypt will have seven good years.
There will be plenty of food to eat.
Then there will be seven bad years.
No food will grow."
The king could tell that Joseph was wise.
So he made Joseph a leader in Egypt.

A Surprise Visit

Joseph helped the people save their food
for seven good years.
Then when the bad years came and no food
grew, the people ate the food they had saved.
No food grew in Canaan
where Joseph's family lived.
But they heard there was food in Egypt.
So his brothers went to Egypt to get food.
They did not know they would
have to buy it from Joseph.

JOSEPH & HIS FAMILY REUNITED, from Genesis 42-46

The brothers bowed to Joseph.
They did not know he was their brother.
But he knew who they were.
Still, he did not tell them he was Joseph.
They asked him for food,
and he sold some to them.

The brothers went back home.
But it wasn't long until
they needed more food.
And they had to go back to Joseph.
They bowed down to him again.
This time, Joseph told them
he was their brother.

What Joseph had dreamed had really happened.
Now his brothers were afraid of him,
because they had been mean to him.
But Joseph said, "Don't be afraid.
God meant it for good."

He kissed all his brothers.
They went home and told their father
that Joseph was all right.
Then their whole family moved to Egypt
to be near Joseph.

A Basket Boat

Now Joseph grew old and died in Egypt.
Many years later, a new king began to rule.
He did not remember Joseph.
He did not like Joseph's family.
He made them do hard work.
He did not even want them to have boy babies.

The people of Joseph's family
were called Israelites.
And the Israelites were afraid
of the mean king.

One Israelite woman had a baby boy.
She wanted to hide him from the king.
So she made a special basket.
It could float.
She put the baby in the basket.
Then she took the basket to the river.
She let it float on the water.

The baby's sister hid
by the river to watch.
She saw the king's daughter, the princess,
come down to the river.
The princess saw the basket.
She opened it and found the baby.
She liked the baby.
She wanted it to be her own baby.

The baby's sister went to the princess.
"Do you want someone to take care
of this baby for you?" she asked.
"Yes," said the princess.
So the sister ran and got her mother
to take care of the baby.

The baby's mother took good care of him.
She took him to the princess
when he was big enough.
The princess named the baby Moses.
Moses grew up in the palace.

The Burning Bush

When Moses grew up, he left the palace.
He did not like to see how the king
made his people work so hard.
He went to another land.
There he took care of sheep.

One day while he was watching the sheep,
he saw a bush covered with fire.
But it did not burn up.
When he went closer to see the bush,
God called him.
"Moses, I want you to go to the king.
Tell him to let my people leave Egypt."

Moses was afraid.
But God said, "I will be with you.
I promise I will bring the people
out of Egypt.
I will lead them to a special land."
But Moses was still afraid.

So God said, "Throw down the rod
you are holding."
Moses threw it down.
It turned into a snake.

God said, "Pick it up again."
Moses picked it up.
It turned back into a rod.
God said, "I will use signs like this
to show the king that I am with you."

So Moses went back to Egypt.
He told his people that God
would take them out of Egypt.
He would lead them to a new land.

Hard Times For Egypt

Moses went to the king of Egypt.
He said, "God wants you to let his people go."
But the king said, "No."

TEN PLAGUES, from Exodus 5-11

So God turned all the water into blood.
The people could not drink the water.
But the king would not let the people go.

God made frogs come all over the land.
Frogs were in ovens, in beds, everywhere.
The king said, "Make the frogs go away.
Then your people can go."
But after God took the frogs away,
the king said, "No, the people cannot go."

God made gnats come all over the land.
The gnats were on people.
They were on animals.
But the king would not let the people go.

Then God sent flies to Egypt.
The houses were full of flies.
The ground was covered with flies.
The king said, "The people can go.
But take away the flies, too!"
So God took the flies away.
But then the king said, "You cannot go."

Then God said, "Your cows and horses and
donkeys will get sick."
And that's what happened.
All the animals got sick.
But the king still would not let them go.

So God made the people of Egypt get sick.
They had sores on their bodies.
But the king would not let the people go.

Then God sent a hailstorm.
Hail beat down everything growing
in the fields.
The king said, "We have had enough.
Take the people and go."
But when he saw the hail stop,
he said, "You cannot go."

So God sent locusts all over Egypt.
They covered the ground until it was black.
They ate the fruit off the trees.
The king said, "Take away these locusts.
Then you can go."
But when the locusts were gone,
he changed his mind again.

Then God sent darkness to cover the land.
Even in the daytime, it was dark.
No one could see anything.
They could not leave their houses.
But the king still would not let them go.

Then God said, "The oldest boy in each family
of the people of Egypt will die.
But my people will be safe."
It happened just as God said.
And that night, the king called Moses.
"Go!" he said.
So God's people took all they had and left.

The Sea Rolls Back

God led the people out of Egypt
by a pillar of cloud in the daytime.
At night, he led them in a pillar of fire.
He led them to the edge of a sea.
Now the king of Egypt sent his army
after the Israelites.
God's people were scared.
The army was chasing them.
But they could not get away because
the sea was in front of them.
Moses said, "Do not be afraid.
God will take care of us."

CROSSING THE RED SEA, from Exodus 14 & 15

God did take care of them.
That night, God sent a strong wind
to push the sea back.
Then God's people could walk
across the sea bed.
On both sides of them,
the sea was pushed back.
They walked across on dry ground!

The army tried to follow them.
They tried to cross the sea, too.
But God made the water pour
back over the sea bed.
The sea covered the whole army.
God saved his people.
They all sang a song of thanks to God.

Manna, Quail, and Water

God's people traveled a long way.
They began to complain.
They said they did not have enough food.
So God sent food to them.
That evening, at dinnertime,
quail came for them to catch and eat.
And at every breakfast time, they found
sweet wafers of bread on the ground.
They called it manna.

The Israelites kept traveling.
Everywhere they went, God gave them manna.
But at one place, there was no water.
The people complained again.
"Give us water to drink," they told Moses.

Moses asked God what to do.
God showed Moses a big rock.
He told Moses to hit the rock with his staff.
Moses did what God told him to do.
Water poured out of the rock.
The people drank all they wanted.

God's Rules

One day, the Israelites camped
near a mountain.
God called Moses up to the mountain.
He wanted to talk to Moses.
The mountain shook.
A thick cloud covered it.
There was thunder and lightning.
God had come to the mountain in the cloud.

Moses went up the mountain.
He talked with God.
God told Moses the rules he wanted
to give to his people.
God said, "Do not kill.
Do not steal.
Respect your father and mother."
He gave them many other rules.

God also told Moses to build
a house of worship.
The people built it just the way
God told them to.
They called the house "the tabernacle."
The cloud that led them covered
the tabernacle.
When the cloud moved, they followed it.
They took the tabernacle with them.
When the cloud stopped, the people stopped.

Twelve Spies

Finally God's people came to the land
God had promised them.
God said, "Send some men into the land
to see what it is like."
So Moses chose twelve men.
He said, "Go into the land.
Then come back and tell us
if it is good or bad.
Are the people strong or weak?"

The men went into the new land.
They brought back some fruit.
They said, "It is a good land.
But the people are strong.
They will fight us and they will win."
The Israelites were afraid.
"We cannot take the land," they said.

Joshua and Caleb said, "Do not be afraid.
God is with us."
But the people would not listen to them.
God was angry with his people.
They did not believe he would help them.
So God said, "You cannot have the land yet.
You will have to travel for 40 more years."
And that's just what they did.

A Talking Donkey

God made his people strong.
Other countries were afraid of them.
The king of Moab was afraid.
He wanted to fight God's people.
But he wanted to be sure he would win.
So he talked to Balaam.
Now Balaam was a man who knew how
to bless or curse people.
When he blessed, or said good things,
good would happen.
When he cursed, or said bad things,
bad would happen.
The king of Moab said he would pay Balaam
to curse God's people.

BALAAM'S BLESSING, from Numbers 22-24

That night, God talked to Balaam.
He told Balaam not to curse his people.
But Balaam went to meet the king.
Now an angel stood in the road to stop him.
Balaam did not see it, but his donkey did.
The donkey walked off the road into a field.
Balaam was angry and hit the donkey.

The donkey moved close to a wall.
Balaam beat his donkey.
Then the donkey just lay down.
Balaam beat the donkey again.
Then God let the donkey talk!
"Why are you beating me?" it said.
"You have made a fool out of me,"
said Balaam.
Then Balaam saw the angel.
He bowed down.

God said, "Why did you beat your donkey?
I sent my angel to stop you.
You are not doing right."
Balaam said, "I have sinned.
Do you want me to go home?"
God said, "Go to the king.
But you must bless my people."
So Balaam met the king, but he blessed
God's people instead of cursing them.

A Wall Falls Down

God gave his people a new leader.
His name was Joshua.
He led God's people to the new land
that God had promised to give them.
The first city they came to was Jericho.
It had a big wall around it.
Joshua sent two men to Jericho
to see what it was like.

The king of Jericho found out
that the men were in his city.
He wanted to catch them.
But they went to the house of a lady
named Rahab.
She hid them on her roof.
The king's men could not find them there.

Rahab's house was part of the city wall.
So when it was night, she let the two men
down through her window by a rope.
They promised that they would help her later,
since she helped them.

The city of Jericho was strong.
But God told Joshua how to take it.
He did just as God told him.
He marched his army around the city
one time each day for six days.
The next day they marched around the city
seven times.

The priests blew their trumpets.
The people shouted.
And the walls around Jericho fell down.
The two men ran back to Rahab's house.
They helped her get out of the city safely.
Then Rahab and her family lived
with God's people.

Trumpets and Torches

After God's people moved into their new land,
many enemies came to fight them.
God chose a man named Gideon
to lead his people.
God said, "You will help save my people."
Gideon set a bundle of wool on the ground.
He said, "If what you say is true, then
in the morning let the wool be wet with dew.
But let the ground be dry."
And it happened just as Gideon asked.

GIDEON, from Judges 6 & 7

Then Gideon said, "God, don't be angry.
But if I will really save your people,
then in the morning let the wool be dry.
And let the ground be wet."
And it happened again just as Gideon asked.

So Gideon chose an army.
Thousands of men were in his army.
But God sent many of them back home.
Finally, Gideon had only 300 men left.

Then God told Gideon how to win the fight
without even fighting!
This is what he did.
Late that night, each man took a torch,
an empty clay jar and a trumpet.
They covered the torches with the jars.
They all crept to the edge of the enemy camp.

When Gideon gave the signal, all his men
blew their trumpets and smashed their jars.
This scared the enemies so much
that they ran away.
God's people won without even fighting!

Long and Strong

It was not long before enemies came again.
So God chose another man to save his people.
His name was Samson.
God had told Samson never to cut his hair.
As long as Samson obeyed God,
he was very strong.

SAMSON, from Judges 13-16

One time Samson spent the night in Gaza.
Around the city was a big wall with a big gate.
The people of Gaza wanted to catch Samson.
But Samson left in the middle of the night.
He tore down the locked gates.
He carried them away on his shoulders.

The enemies asked a lady named Delilah
to find out how to make Samson weak.
So she asked Samson how.
He said, "Tie me with seven cords."
That night the enemies tied him
with seven cords.
But when Samson woke up,
he snapped them right off.

So Delilah kept asking Samson
why he was so strong.
Finally Samson said, "If you cut my hair
I will be weak."
That night, while he was asleep,
Delilah called a man to cut his hair.
He was not strong anymore.
The enemies took him and put him in jail.

But God still let Samson win.
It happened when the enemies
were having a party in a big house.
They took Samson with them to the party.
God gave him strength.
Samson pushed down the pillars that
held up the roof.
The roof fell in on top of all the enemies.
God had saved his people again.

Ruth

Ruth lived far away from Judah,
the land of God's people.
But she lived with Naomi,
who had come from Judah.
Ruth had married Naomi's son.
But he had died.
Naomi's husband had died, too.
Now Naomi wanted to go back to Judah.

"Go back to your mother and father,"
Naomi told Ruth.
But Ruth said, "Please take me with you.
I will go where you go.
I will stay where you stay.
Your people will be my people.
Your God will be my God."
So Naomi took Ruth with her to Judah.

In Judah, Ruth had to work to get food
for them to eat.
She worked in the fields.
She picked up the grain
that was left over after the harvest.

The farmer of that field was named Boaz.
Boaz knew that Ruth was helping Naomi.
He told his farm helpers to leave grain
especially for Ruth.
He was glad she was picking up grain
in his field.
And Ruth knew that Boaz was a kind man.

Boaz fell in love with Ruth.
He married her.
They had a baby named Obed.
And they were happy together.

A Special Prayer

There was once a woman named Hannah.
Hannah was very sad,
because she had no children.
She wanted a baby very much.
One day she and her husband
went to worship God at the tabernacle.
Hannah prayed to God there.
She cried and said, "If you will give me
a baby, I will let him work for you
all his life."

HANNAH, from 1 Samuel 1 & 2

The priest, named Eli, saw Hannah.
He knew something was wrong.
Hannah told him what she was doing.
He said, "Go home in peace.
May God give you what you have asked him for."

Hannah did go home.
And God remembered her prayer.
He gave Hannah a baby boy.
She named him Samuel.

A Voice at Night

When Samuel was old enough, his mother
took him to live with Eli at the tabernacle.
One night after they had gone to bed,
Samuel heard a voice calling him.
Now Samuel thought it was Eli.
So he ran to Eli.
"Here I am," said Samuel.
But Eli said, "I did not call you.
Go back to bed."
Samuel went back to bed.

SAMUEL, from 1 Samuel 3

Then he heard it again: "Samuel!"
Samuel got up.
He ran to Eli.
"Here I am," he said.
"I did not call you," said Eli.
"Go back to bed."

But Samuel heard it again: "Samuel!"
Samuel ran to Eli.
"Here I am," he said.
Then Eli knew that God was calling.
He said, "Go and lie down.
If you hear the voice again,
say 'Speak Lord, I am listening.'"
So Samuel lay down in his bed.

Soon God called again: "Samuel! Samuel!"
Samuel said, "Speak Lord, I am listening."
And God spoke to Samuel.
From then on, God talked to Samuel.
Samuel told God's people what God said.
Samuel was a prophet.

The First King

God's people did not have a king.
God led them by his prophet Samuel.
But the people said,
"Give us a king to lead us."
Samuel asked God about it.

God said, "Give them a king.
But tell them they will be sorry.
They will have to obey their king.
He might make them do things
they do not want to do."
Samuel told the people what God said.
But still they wanted a king.

So God chose a king for them.
His name was Saul.
He was a tall man.
But he was a shy man.

When it was time for him to become king,
Saul hid.
But the people found him.
They brought him out in front of everyone.
They all shouted, "Long live the king!"

At first, Saul was a good king.
But then he stopped obeying God.
So God told Samuel
he wanted a new king for his people.

A Good Heart

God told Samuel to go to Jesse's house.
Jesse had eight sons.
God wanted one of these sons
to be the new king.
Jesse called his sons together.
Samuel looked at the first one.
"This is surely the one God has chosen,"
he thought.
But God said, "No, you are thinking about
what he looks like.
I am looking at his heart."

DAVID CHOSEN KING, from 1 Samuel 16

So Samuel looked at Jesse's sons, one by one.
But God had not chosen any of them.
"Do you have any more sons?" Samuel asked.
"There is one more," said Jesse.
"But he is keeping the sheep."
"Tell him to come," said Samuel.

When he came, God said, "This is the one."
His name was David.
Samuel told David that one day
he would be the new king.

The Giant

The enemies of God's people came out to fight.
They sent their best fighter out first.
His name was Goliath.
He was over nine feet tall.
He called to the army of Saul,
"Choose a man to come and fight me.
If he wins, we will be your servants.
But if I win, you will be our servants!"
The men in Saul's army were afraid.
They knew Goliath was stronger than they were.
No one wanted to fight him.

DAVID & GOLIATH, from 1 Samuel 17

Now David's brothers were in Saul's army.
But David was at home keeping the sheep.
One day, David's father called him.
"Take this bread to your brothers," he said.
So David got to go to his brothers.
He got to see the army.

He also got to see Goliath.
And he saw how everyone was afraid of him.
"I will fight Goliath," said David.
But Saul said, "You are only a boy.
How can you fight Goliath?"
"God will help me," said David.

So Saul gave David his armor and helmet.
He gave him a sword.
David tried them on.
But they were too heavy.
David gave them back to Saul.
"I am not used to these," he said.

Instead, David chose five smooth stones
from a stream.
He took his sling in his hand.
David called to Goliath, "You come
with a sword and a spear.
But I come to you in the name of God.
This battle is the Lord's."

The giant came closer to fight David.
But David put a stone in his sling.
He threw the stone at Goliath.

The stone hit Goliath right in his forehead.
And Goliath fell down.
David trusted God.
God helped David win.
All the people were glad.

Best Friends

David had a special job at Saul's house.
When Saul felt bad,
David played music for him.
Then Saul would feel better.

DAVID & JONATHAN, from 1 Samuel 18-20

Now Saul had a son.

His name was Jonathan.

Jonathan liked David very much.

He gave David his robe and tunic.

He gave David his bow, his belt,
and his sword.

They became best friends.

God blessed David.
Whenever David went to fight, he won.
The people began to like David
better than Saul.
This made Saul jealous and angry.

Saul got so angry at David,
he threw his spear at him.
He tried to kill David.
But David ran from Saul.

Jonathan said, "You must leave
this city, David.
Get away from Saul."
David was sad.
He would miss Jonathan.
But Jonathan said,
"We will always be friends.
We are best friends forever."

King David

Saul chased David.
But he never caught him.
God was taking care of David.
After Saul died, David became the king.
David was a good king.
He loved God.
He wrote songs about his love for God.

David wrote, "The Lord is my shepherd.
I shall not want.
He makes me lie down in green pastures.
He leads me beside still waters."

He wrote, "Praise the Lord.
Praise him, sun and moon.
Praise him, all you shining stars.
Praise him, snow and clouds.
Praise him, mountains and trees.
Praise him, animals.
Praise him, old men and children.
Praise the Lord."

Solomon

King David had a son named Solomon.
Solomon grew up to be the king after David.
One night, God asked Solomon
"What would you like to have, Solomon?"
Solomon said, "I just want to be wise."
God said, "I will give you a wise heart."

So Solomon was the wisest king in the world.
Many people came to ask him questions
and hear him teach.
God also made Solomon very rich.
And God's people did not have enemies.
They all lived in peace.

Then Solomon chose workers
to build a special house.
It was a beautiful temple for God.
It was a place where the people could worship.

And when it was finished,
Solomon lifted his hands to heaven.
"Praise the Lord," he said.
"He has kept all of his promises.
May he be with us forever."

Food from Birds

After Solomon, many kings were bad.
They forgot God.
They began to worship statues
made of stone and wood.
God was very unhappy about this.

So God chose a man to remind the kings
that he was the only true God.
Elijah was the man God chose.
Elijah was a prophet.
He told the kings what God wanted them to do.

Ahab was one of those mean kings.
He would not even listen to Elijah.
He did not want to do what God wanted.
Elijah said, "Because you are a bad king,
no rain will come for a long time."

Since there was no rain,
there was not much food.
Even Elijah had no food.
But God took care of Elijah.
He showed Elijah a brook
where he could get water.
Elijah lived by the brook.

Ravens brought him bread and meat
every morning.
They brought him bread and meat
every evening.
And Elijah drank water from the brook.

A Jar and a Jug

Since there was no rain,
Elijah's brook dried up.
He had no water.
He had no food.
But still God took care of him.
"Go to a small town in Sidon," said God.
"A lady there will give you food."

So Elijah went.
At the town gate, he saw a lady.
"Will you bring me some water and bread?"
Elijah asked.

The lady said, "I only have a little flour
in a jar.
I have a little oil in a jug.
I was going to make some bread
for me and my son.
It is all we have."

But Elijah said, "Do not be afraid.
Make me some bread first.
Then make some for you and your son.
God will not let the jar of flour be empty.
He will not let the jug run out of oil."

The lady did what Elijah told her.
And God kept his promise.
Her jar of flour was not used up.
Her jug of oil was never empty.
So there was food for her family every day.
Elijah stayed at her house.
And she shared her food with Elijah.

The True God

Mean king Ahab kept on being mean.
He built statues of wood and metal and stone.
He called them Baals.
He said that Baal was God.
He wanted all the people to worship Baal.
God sent Elijah to the people.
Elijah said, "Who is the true God?
We can find out."

ELIJAH ON MOUNT CARMEL, from 1 Kings 18

"We will build two altars of stone.
One will be for Baal.
One will be for my God.
We will put wood on the altars.
Then we will pray for God
to send fire to burn the wood."
So they followed Elijah's plan.

The followers of Baal prayed to Baal.

They asked him to send fire.

But Baal was only a statue.

He could not hear them.

No fire came.

"Call louder," said Elijah.

"Maybe he is busy, or gone on a trip.

Maybe he is asleep."

So they yelled and shouted, but no fire came.

Now it was Elijah's turn.

He dug a ditch around his altar.

He poured a lot of water on the altar.

The wood got wet.

The altar got wet.

Water filled the ditch.

Then Elijah prayed.
"Oh God, show the people
that you are the true God."
And God sent fire!
It burned up the wood and the altar.
It even burned up the water in the ditch!
Then everyone knew who was the true God!

The Chariot of Fire

Elijah wanted a helper.
So he chose a man to help him.
This man's name was Elisha.
Elisha loved God, too.
One day Elijah took Elisha with him
on a long walk.
Elijah was an old man now.
It was time for him to go to heaven.

When they came to the Jordan River,
Elijah took his cloak off.
He hit the water with it.
The water moved back on each side.
Elijah and Elisha walked across on dry land.

Then Elijah asked, "What can I do
for you before I go?"
"I want to be like you," said Elisha.
"You have asked a hard thing," said Elijah.
"But if you see me go,
you will get what you asked for."

As they were walking and talking,
they saw a chariot of fire coming.
Horses of fire pulled it.
It came between Elijah and Elisha.
And Elijah went up to heaven in a whirlwind.
Elisha watched.

Then Elisha picked up Elijah's cloak.
He walked back to the river.
He hit the river with the cloak.
And the water moved back
so he could walk across.
Elisha now had God's power with him
just like Elijah had.

Jars of Oil

One day a woman came to Elisha.
She was worried.
"I don't have the money I need
to pay for everything I have.
The man I owe is angry.
He will take my two sons.
He will make them work for him.
What can I do?"
Elisha asked, "What do you have at home?"
"I only have a little oil," she said.

Elisha said, "Ask your neighbors
for empty jars.
Then pour oil into each jar."
The woman did what Elisha told her.
She poured and poured.
Still her oil did not run out.
Her oil was not gone
until she had filled all the jars.

She told Elisha, "All the jars are full."
Elisha said, "Go and sell the oil.
Take the money you get and pay back
what you owe.
You can keep the money that is left over."

A Room on the Roof

Elisha went many places
doing what God wanted.
One day he went to Shunem.
A rich woman lived there.
She took Elisha to her house for dinner.
From then on, when he was in Shunem,
he ate at her house.
They were good friends.

ELISHA & THE SHUNEMITE WOMAN, from 2 Kings 4

229

"Let's make a room for Elisha on our roof,"
the woman told her husband.
"We will put a bed in it.
We will put a table, a chair and a lamp in it.
He can stay there whenever he comes to visit."
So they made a room for Elisha.

Now Elisha had a helper.
And one day when Elisha was staying in Shunem,
he asked his helper,
"What can I do for this woman?
She has made this room for me."
"She has no son," his helper said.

So Elisha called the woman.
"Next year," he said, "God will give you
a baby boy."
It happened just as Elisha had said.
The next year she did have a baby boy.
And she loved him very much.

Naaman

Naaman was the leader of a great army.
His wife had a little servant girl
from Israel.
But Naaman was sad and worried.
He had a sickness called leprosy.
It was a very bad sickness.

HEALED OF LEPROSY, from 2 Kings 5

One day the servant girl
said to Naaman's wife,
"I wish Naaman would go see Elisha.
Elisha would help him get well."

So Naaman went to Elisha's house.
And Elisha told him, "Go to the Jordan River.
Wash yourself seven times there.
Then you will be well."

This sounded silly to Naaman.
He was angry.
"I could wash in my own rivers at home,"
he said.
"They are better."

But Naaman's servants said,
"Do what Elisha said.
It is an easy thing to do."
So Naaman went to the Jordan River.
He washed seven times.
And he was well,
just as Elisha said he would be.

A Boy King

Josiah was eight years old
when he became king.
He was a good king.
He obeyed God.
Parts of God's temple
were broken and old.
Josiah got workers
to build it back.

One day, the priest found something
in the temple.
It was something important.
It was the Book of the Law of God.
It had been forgotten for many years.

He took the book to King Josiah.
The king read it.
"We must follow these laws," he said.
"We must do what God wants."
And they did.
God was happy with King Josiah.
And God blessed him.

Food for Daniel

One day the army of Babylon
came to fight God's people.
They took some things from God's temple.
And they took some of the young men
from the king's palace.
Four of these young men were Daniel
and his friends Shadrach, Meshach,
and Abednego.

YOUNG CAPTIVES IN BABYLON, from Daniel 1

Now the king of Babylon wanted
these young men to be his helpers.
He told his special servant
to give them food from his table.
Daniel knew that the king's food
would not be good for them.
He asked the servant not to give
them the king's food.

"If you do not eat the king's food,
you will be sick and not strong.
The king will be angry," said the servant.
But Daniel said, "Give us vegetables
and water for ten days.
Then see if we are sick or not."

So the servant did what Daniel asked.
He gave them vegetables to eat.
He gave them water to drink.
At the end of ten days,
the servant was surprised.
They looked strong, not sick.
They looked better than the men
who ate the king's food.

God blessed Daniel and his friends.
They were far away from home,
But God was still with them.
God made them know and understand
many things.
And they loved and obeyed God.

In the Fire

One day, the king of Babylon set up
a tall, gold statue.
He told the people,
"Horns and pipes will play.
When you hear the music, bow down.
Worship the statue.
If you don't I will throw you
into a big fire."
Shadrach, Meshach and Abednego knew
they could only worship the true God.
They heard the music.
But they did not bow down.

Someone told the king.

He called Shadrach, Meshach and Abednego.

"Bow down and worship the statue," he said.

But they said,

"We will never worship a statue."

The king was very angry.
He called his servants.
"Make the fire as hot as you can.
And throw these men into it," he said.
So his helpers made a hot, hot fire.
They threw Shadrach, Meshach and Abednego
into the fire.

But the king could not believe his eyes.
Suddenly there were four men in the fire.
One looked like a son of God.
They were walking around.
They were not burning!

"Come out!" the king called.

Shadrach, Meshach, and Abednego came out.

They were not burned.

They did not even smell like smoke!

The king was amazed.

He praised God.

He knew God had saved them.

Spending the Night with Lions

God blessed Daniel.

He made Daniel very wise.

The king planned to make Daniel
ruler of all the land.

Now the other wise men were jealous.

They tried to find something bad about Daniel.

But Daniel was a good man.

He always prayed to God.

He always obeyed God.

The men could not find anything bad.

So they made a plan.

They went to the king.
"Let's make a new law," they said.
"Let's say that everyone has to pray to you.
If they don't, we will throw them
into the lions' den."
That sounded good to the king.
He made it a new law.

Daniel heard about the new law.
But he went to his room and prayed anyway.
Now the men knew Daniel would pray.
They saw him and took him to the king.
"Let's throw Daniel into the lions' den,"
they said.

The king was sorry.
He liked Daniel.
But he could not change his law.
The men's plan had worked.
They threw Daniel to the lions.

The next morning, the king got up early.

He ran to the lions' den.

"Daniel, did God save you?" he called.

"Yes, king," said Daniel.

"God sent an angel to close the lions' mouths."

The king was happy.

He took Daniel out.

God had saved him.

Inside a Fish

One day God spoke to a man named Jonah.
"You must go to the city of Ninevah,"
God said.
"They are doing bad things there.
You must tell them to stop."

Jonah did not obey God.

He got on a big ship.

He tried to sail away from God.

But God knew where Jonah was.

He sent a big storm.

"Why has a storm come?" asked the sailors.

"It came because of me," said Jonah.

"If you throw me into the sea, it will stop."

So they threw Jonah into the sea.
And the storm did stop.
But a big fish swam up and swallowed Jonah.
Inside the fish, Jonah prayed and prayed.
After three days and nights, God saved him.
He made that fish spit Jonah out on the land.

Then God said, "Jonah, go to Ninevah!"
And Jonah went!
He told the people to stop being bad.
The people listened to Jonah.
And they started doing good things.
God was glad that Jonah had obeyed.

Timeless Stories
from the NEW TESTAMENT

The Angel's Secret

Gabriel was an angel.
He obeyed God.
Sometimes he took special news
from God to people on earth.

GABRIEL VISITS MARY, from Luke 1

One day God sent Gabriel to a young lady.
Her name was Mary.
Gabriel went to Mary.
He said, "Greetings!
God is with you!"

Mary was afraid.

She wondered what he meant.

But Gabriel said, "Do not be afraid.

God loves you.

He is going to give you a baby.

You will name him Jesus.

He will be God's Son!"

Mary was surprised.
"How can this be true?" she asked.
"Nothing is impossible with God,"
said Gabriel.

"I believe you," said Mary.
"I will do whatever God wants."
Then Gabriel left Mary.

The Most Special Baby

Now Mary loved a man named Joseph.
They were going to get married.
One day Joseph had to take a trip
to the city of Bethlehem.
So Mary went with him.

The city of Bethlehem was crowded.
Many people had come there.
Joseph and Mary looked for a place to stay.
But there was no room in any house.

All the beds were full.
People were even sleeping on the floors.
So Joseph and Mary had to stay in a stable
where the donkeys and horses stayed.

That night, the baby was born.

It was God's baby son.

Mary and Joseph named him Jesus,

just as the angel had told them to do.

They wrapped him up so he would be warm.

Mary made a soft bed for him in a manger.
The baby Jesus slept there.
Mary loved him.
Joseph loved him.
And God loved him.

Good News

It was still night.
Outside the town of Bethlehem,
some sheep were sleeping.
Shepherds were watching them.
Suddenly an angel came to the shepherds.
And God's glory shone around them.
They were afraid.

THE ANGELS & THE SHEPHERDS, from Luke 2

But the angel said, "Do not be afraid.
I am bringing you good news.
This is happy news for all the people:
today in Bethlehem, God's Son was born.
You can go see him.
He is wrapped warm and snug in a manger!"

Then many, many angels came from heaven.
They praised God.
"Glory to God in the highest,
and peace on earth!"

When the angels left, the shepherds said,
"Let's go find this baby!"
So they hurried to town.
They found the stable.
And they saw the new baby.

Then the shepherds left, thanking God.
They told everyone what had happened.
The people were amazed.
And Mary always remembered this special time.

Blessings for the Baby

Soon after Jesus was born,
Joseph and Mary took him to the temple.
There was an old man there named Simeon.
He was waiting to see baby Jesus.
He knew Jesus was special.
He held Jesus in his arms.
He thanked God for baby Jesus.

SIMEON & ANNA, from Luke 2

There was also an old woman at the temple.
Her name was Anna.
She also knew Jesus was special.

She came to Mary and Joseph.
She was happy to see baby Jesus.
She, too, thanked God for baby Jesus.

Visitors from the East

God put a special star in the sky
when Jesus was born.
Some wise men who lived in the east
saw this star.
They knew it was a sign.
It meant that a baby king had been born.
These wise men wanted to visit the baby.
So they followed the star for a long way.

THE WISE MEN FIND JESUS, from Matthew 2

The wise men went to King Herod in Jerusalem.
"We know a baby king was born," they said.
"Can you tell us where he is?"
This worried the king.
He did not like anyone else
to be called the king.

He did not know this baby king
was the king of heaven and earth.
He did not know this baby king was God's Son.
"I do not know this new king,"
said King Herod.
"But go and find him.
Then tell me where he is."

So the wise men went on.
And the star led them right to the place
where Jesus was.
They were very happy they had found him.
They bowed down.
They gave him gifts: sweet-smelling gifts,
sparkling, golden gifts.

God knew King Herod did not like
anyone else to be called the king.
God sent the wise men a dream.
This dream told them not to tell King Herod
where the baby was.
So the wise men went home a different way.

Running Away

The wise men did not go back to King Herod.
King Herod was upset.
He wanted to find the baby king.
He wanted to kill him.
Herod wanted to be the only king around.

But God knew what King Herod was thinking.
God sent an angel to Joseph in a dream.
The angel said, "Run away to Egypt.
Stay there until I say you can come back."

So Joseph and Mary and baby Jesus
went to Egypt.
They lived there until King Herod died.
Then an angel came again to Joseph.
"You can move back home," he said.
"It is safe now."

Joseph took Mary and Jesus back.
They moved to the town of Nazareth.
Jesus grew up in Nazareth.
God made him strong and wise.

The Man Who Could Not Talk

Zechariah worked in God's temple.
He loved God.
His wife Elizabeth loved God.
They were very old.
But they had no children.

One day at the temple,
an angel came to Zechariah.
The angel said, "I am Gabriel.
I have good news.
You and Elizabeth will have a baby.
You will call him John.
He will be filled with God's Holy Spirit.
He will be a special man."

Zechariah said, "How do I know this is true?"
"You will not be able to speak
until all of this happens," said Gabriel.
"Then you will know that this is true."

When Zechariah came out of the temple,
he could not talk.
He could only move his hands
to tell what he wanted to say.

It all happened as the angel said.
Zechariah and Elizabeth did have a baby.
Everyone wanted to name him Zechariah
like his father.
But Zechariah shook his head.
He remembered what the angel told him.
He wrote on a tablet: "His name is John."
Then God made him able to talk again.
And Zechariah praised God.

Lost!

Jesus grew up in Nazareth.
When Jesus was 12 years old,
Mary and Joseph took him to the temple.
The temple was in Jerusalem.
They had to travel there by walking.
They went with many of their friends
and family.

THE BOY JESUS IN THE TEMPLE, from Luke 2

There were many people in Jerusalem.
It was crowded.
Jesus had a good time there
with friends and family.
But when it was time to go home,
Jesus stayed in Jerusalem.

Mary and Joseph thought he was walking
with his friends.
That night, they looked for him.
When they could not find him,
they were worried.
Jesus was lost!
They hurried back to Jerusalem.

For three days they hunted for Jesus.
At last they found him.
He was in the temple.
He was listening to the wise teachers there.
And he was asking them questions.

Mary said, "We have been worried about you."
Jesus said, "I had to come
to my Father's house."
Jesus knew that God was his Father.
He had been talking to the teachers about God.
But he went home with Mary and Joseph.
And he obeyed them.
God blessed Jesus, and he grew wise and strong.

In the Jordan River

Zechariah and Elizabeth's baby John grew up.
He lived in the desert.
His clothes were made of camel's hair.
He wore a leather belt.
And he ate locusts and wild honey.
He told the people about God.
He also told them that a special man
would come soon: Jesus, the Son of God.

JOHN BAPTIZES JESUS, from Luke 3

Many people listened to John.
John told them to stop doing bad
and to start doing good.

He baptized people in the Jordan River.
He dipped them quickly under the water.
This showed everyone that they
wanted to follow God.
They wanted to stop being bad.
They wanted to start being good.

One day Jesus came to the river.
Jesus asked John to baptize him.
John knew Jesus was the Son of God.
John said, "You are greater than I am.
You should baptize me."
But Jesus said, "No.
I want to do everything that is right."
So John baptized Jesus.

As soon as Jesus came up out of the water,
the Spirit of God came down from heaven.
It looked like a dove.
It landed on Jesus.
And God said, "This is my Son.
I love him.
I am pleased with him."

Helpers and Friends

Jesus knew that he had much work to do.
He wanted to have some good friends
who could help him.
One day Jesus was walking
by the Sea of Galilee.
He saw two boats there.
Peter and Andrew were fishing from one boat.
James and John were mending a net
in the other boat.
Jesus called to them, "Come and follow me."
And they did.

Later, Jesus passed by a tax office.
There was a man there named Matthew.
Matthew's job was to take the taxes,
the money the people paid to the king.
Jesus looked at Matthew.
"Follow me," Jesus said.
Matthew got up and followed Jesus.

Jesus asked twelve men to be his helpers.
Besides Peter, Andrew, James, John and
Matthew, he called Philip, Bartholomew,
Thomas, another man named James,
Simon, Thaddaeus and Judas.

A Wedding Party

One day, Jesus and his helper friends
went to a wedding party.
It was a happy time for everyone.
There was food to eat and wine to drink.

But Jesus' mother came over to him.
"Something terrible has happened," she said.
"They have run out of wine!"
Then she looked at the servants.
"Do whatever Jesus tells you," she said.

There were six very big stone jars nearby.
Jesus told the servants, "Fill those jars
with water."
So the servants filled the jars to the top.
"Now dip some out," said Jesus.
"Give it to the people."

The servants dipped out the water.
But it was not water anymore!
It was wine!

The people drank it.
Some of them said it was the best wine
at the party.
They did not know it had been
plain water.
But the servants knew.
God had given Jesus special power,
because Jesus was God's Son.

Through the Roof

Crowds of people went to see Jesus.
They listened to him teach.
He even healed the sick people.
One day, Jesus was teaching inside a house.
So many people came to see him,
that the house was full.

Four men came with their friend.
Their friend could not walk.
They had to carry him on a little bed.
But they could not get to Jesus.
The house was too full.

That did not stop them.
There were some stairs outside the house.
Up the stairs they went to the roof.
They took off some tiles of the roof
and made a hole.
Then they let their friend down
right through the roof,
right in front of Jesus.

When Jesus saw the man,
he said, "Get up and walk."
The man stood up.
He walked home praising God.
Everybody else was amazed.
They thanked God, too.

On a Mountain

Old men went to see Jesus.
Children went to see Jesus.
Young men and women,
mothers and fathers went to see Jesus.

SERMON ON THE MOUNT, from Matthew 5 & 6

Happy people, sad people, well people,
sick people went to see Jesus.
They wanted to hear what Jesus said.

Jesus saw the people coming.
So he went up the side of a mountain.
He sat down.
"Look at the birds," he said.
"Do they have barns
where they keep their food?
No, God feeds them."

"And look at the flowers.
They do not work.
They do not make clothes to wear.
God dresses them in clothes
more beautiful than a king's."

"You are more important than birds.
You are more important than flowers.
So do not worry.
If God takes care of them,
he will take care of you."

A Sick Servant

There was once a captain in an army.
Many men had to obey him,
because he was in charge.
He was the boss.
Now there was one man
who was very special to the captain.
This man was his helper, his servant.

One day the servant got very sick.

He could not move.

He was hurting.

The captain was sad to see his servant sick.

But the captain knew about Jesus.

He knew that Jesus could make people well.
So the captain found Jesus.
"Lord," he said, "My servant is sick.
He is hurting."
Jesus said, "I will go and make him well."

But the captain said,
"You do not have to come.
Just say the word and my servant will be well.
I know, because I am in charge of many men.
They do what I tell them to do.
You are in charge of this sickness.
It will do what you tell it to do."

Jesus was amazed, because the captain
knew that Jesus had such power.
The captain believed.
"Go back home," Jesus said.
"Your servant will be well."
The captain went home.
And, just as Jesus had said,
his servant *was* well!

The Farmer's Seeds

Jesus liked to tell the people stories.
His stories had special meanings.
One day, he told this story.
"Once there was a farmer.
He went to his field to plant his seeds.
He scattered the seeds here and there.

343

Now some of the seeds fell on the path.
The birds flew down and ate those seeds.
Some of the seeds fell in rocky dirt.
They sprouted, but there were too many rocks.
The roots could not grow and get water.
So when the sun grew hot on them, they died.

Some seeds fell where there were weeds.
The seeds sprouted, but the weeds grew bigger
and crowded them out.
Other seeds fell into good dirt.
There were no weeds or rocks.
They settled deep into the dirt
where no birds could get them.
And they grew and grew and grew."

The people wondered about this story.
"What does it mean?" they asked Jesus.
And Jesus told them.
"The seed is the news about God.
The birds and weeds and rocks
are like some people's hearts.
They hear God's word,
but they have their hearts on other things.

They do not understand.
They do not love God and follow him.
But the good dirt is like the hearts
of people who do understand.
They love God.
God's love grows in their hearts
like a beautiful, healthy plant."

A Tiny Seed and a Big Tree

Many people came to hear Jesus' stories.
Jesus told stories about God's kingdom.
God's kingdom is wherever God is king.
And wherever God is king,
his love will be found.

349

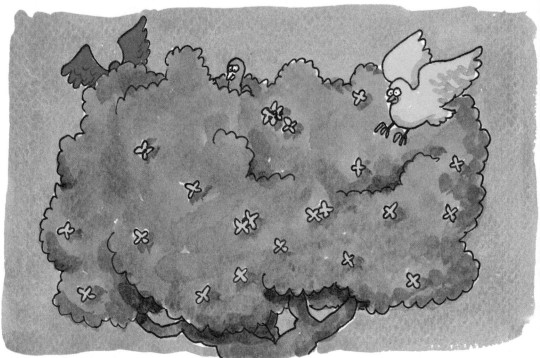

Jesus said God's kingdom is like
a mustard seed.
It is one of the smallest seeds in the world.
But it grows and grows and grows!
And when it is grown, it is one of the
biggest plants in the garden.
It is so big that birds come and rest on its
branches.

God's kingdom can start very small.
God's love may be in only one person's heart.
But when his love is shared,
his kingdom grows and grows and grows!
More and more people want to follow God.

Jesus told another story.

He said God's kingdom is like yeast.

Bakers use yeast to make dough puff up.

Then it will make soft, fluffy
loaves of bread.

Jesus said God's kingdom is like yeast.

A woman mixed the yeast with flour.

She made dough.

The yeast made the dough grow big and puffy.

God's love can start small like yeast.
It can mix into our hearts.
There it grows bigger and bigger.
Soon we have enough love to share
with everyone.

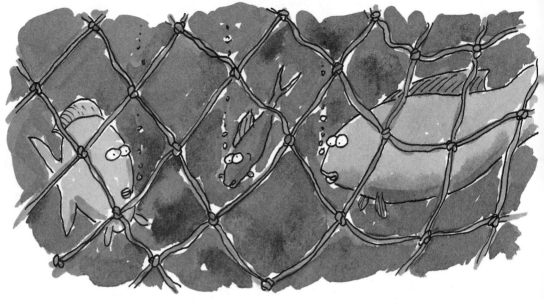

The Net

"Once there was a fisherman," said Jesus.
"He threw out his net.
Down, down it went into the lake.
Soon the fish began to swim around the net.
Many fish swam into the net.
The fisherman waited and watched.
When the net was full,
he pulled it up onto the shore.

PARABLES OF THE KINGDOM, from Matthew 13

"Then he sat down and sorted the fish.
He tossed the good fish into the baskets.
But he threw the bad fish away."

"God's kingdom is like the net," said Jesus.
"Many people will come to it.
One day the angels will sort the people.
The good people will get to stay
in God's kingdom, but the bad people will not."

The Treasure and the Pearl

"God's kingdom is like a treasure," said Jesus.

It is like a treasure hidden in a field.

A man was working in the field.

He did not know about the treasure.

Tap, tap.

His shovel bumped something.

He looked at it.

He dusted it off.

It was real treasure!
He was so excited!
He quickly hid the treasure again.
Then he sold everything he had.
He took the money and bought the field.
Then he ran back and dug up the treasure.

"God's kingdom is like a man who
buys and sells," said Jesus.
This man looks for good things
people would like to buy.
He gets those things and sells them to people.
One day this man was looking for pearls.
He looked and looked.
Then he saw it!

It was a perfect, beautiful pearl!
And it cost a lot of money.
But the man did not care.
He sold everything else he had.
He took the money and bought the pearl.
God's kingdom is the real treasure.
God's kingdom is perfect like the pearl.
It is better than anything else in the world.
It is worth anything you might give up for it.

Wind and Waves

It was late in the day.
Jesus was teaching by the lake.
Many people had come to see him.
And Jesus was tired.
"Let's go to the other side
of the lake," he said to his friends.

JESUS STILLS THE STORM, from Matthew 8, Mark 4, & Luke 8

So they got into their boat.
They started to sail across the lake.
The boat rocked gently up and down.

But the wind began to blow stronger.
The waves began to crash into the boat.
It bobbed high and then dipped low.
Water sloshed into the boat!
Everyone was afraid.
Everyone but Jesus.

Jesus was asleep on a pillow
in the back of the boat.
His friends woke him up.
"Jesus! Don't you hear the wind howling?
Can't you feel the boat tossing?
We are all going to drown!"
"Why are you afraid?" Jesus asked.

Then he looked at the wind and the stormy sea.
"Peace!" he said. "Be still."
The wind stopped blowing.
The waves stopped crashing.
Everything was quiet and still.
Jesus' friends were amazed.
"Even the wind and the waves obey Jesus,"
they said.

One Touch

People crowded around Jesus as he walked.
They pushed this way and that.
They even bumped into Jesus.
Some people just wanted to see
what Jesus looked like.
Some wanted to talk to him.
Some wanted to listen to him.

One woman wanted Jesus to make her well.
She had been sick for twelve years.
She had spent all her money
going to see doctors.
No one could make her better.
She kept thinking, "If I could only
get to Jesus!
If I could just touch his clothes!"

She pushed closer and closer.
Finally she was close enough.
She reached out—she touched his cloak!
Right away she felt better!
She knew she was well!

Jesus stopped walking.

He turned around.

"Who touched me?" he asked.

"All these people are crowding around you,"
Peter said.

"Many people touched you."

"But I felt some power go out of me,"
Jesus said.

Then the woman came to Jesus.

"I touched you," she said.

"And you are well now, because you believed," said Jesus.

"Go in peace."

A Big Picnic

More than 10 people,
more than 50 people,
more than 100 people,
more than 1,000 people,
5,000 people had come to hear Jesus.
They stayed all afternoon.
At dinnertime, they were still listening
to Jesus.

JESUS FEEDS THE FIVE THOUSAND, from Matthew 14, Mark 6, & Luke 9

Jesus' friends said, "Let's tell
these people to leave now.
They can go and get something to eat."
"They do not need to go," said Jesus.
"But we do not have the money
to buy food for them," said Philip.

"You are right," said Andrew.
"And I only know one person who brought food.
A little boy here has five loaves of bread
and two fish.
That is not enough to feed 5,000 people!"

But Jesus said, "Tell the people to sit down."
Everyone sat down on the soft grass.
Jesus took the five loaves and the two fish.
He prayed and thanked God for the food.
Then his friends began to give food
to the people.

Now, there were not only five loaves
and two fish.
There was plenty of bread and fish
for everyone.
Each person got to eat as much as he wanted.

Walking on Water

Night was coming.
Jesus was tired.
It had been a very busy day.
Jesus wanted to be alone for awhile.
He wanted to pray.
While he went up into the hills,
his friends got into their boat.
They started rowing to the other side
of the lake.

MIRACLE ON THE SEA OF GALILEE, *from Matthew 14*

The wind was blowing against them.
It pushed their boat back.
Jesus saw that they were having
a hard time rowing.
So he came to them walking on the water!
When they saw him, they were scared.
They did not know it was Jesus.

Jesus knew they were scared.
"Do not be afraid," he said, "It is I."
Peter wanted to make sure this was true.
"If it really is you," he said,
"tell me to come to you on the water."
"Come on," said Jesus.

Peter got out of the boat.

Step, step, step.

He began to walk on the water, too!

But then he felt the strong wind.

He looked at the waves.

He began to sink.

"Jesus, save me!" he cried.

Right away, Jesus pulled Peter up.

"Why did you get scared?" Jesus asked.

Then they climbed into the boat.

The wind stopped blowing.

Everyone worshipped Jesus.

"You really *are* God's Son," they said.

Open Eyes

He could not see flowers.
He could not see people.
He could not see anything.
He had been blind ever since he was born.
But something special happened
to this blind man:
Jesus saw him.

JESUS HEALS A BLIND MAN, from John 9

Jesus did something strange.
He spit on the dirt and made some mud.
Then he put the mud on the man's eyes.
"Go and wash your eyes," Jesus said.

The man did what Jesus said.
He washed the mud off his eyes.
He looked around.
He could see!
And the man worshipped Jesus.

Money in a Fish

In the land where Jesus lived,
everyone had to pay money to their king.
This money was called the tax.
The men who took the money
were called tax collectors.

One day the tax collectors came to Peter.
"Does Jesus pay the tax money?" they asked.
"Yes," Peter answered, "he does."
Then he went to find Jesus.

But Jesus already knew
about the tax collectors.
He knew what to do.
"Go fishing at the lake," said Jesus.
"When you catch your first fish,
look in its mouth."

So Peter went fishing.
He looked into the mouth of his first fish.
Inside its mouth, he found some money!
He took that money to the tax collectors.
There was plenty to pay Jesus' tax
and Peter's tax.

A Good Neighbor

"I know that I should love God,"
a man once said to Jesus.
"I should love him with all my heart.
And I should love my neighbor, too.
But who is my neighbor?"
Jesus told him this story.

THE GOOD SAMARITAN, from Luke 10

There was a man walking along a road.
He was going on a trip.
Suddenly, robbers jumped out at him.
They hit him.
They took all the things he had with him.
And they left him, hurt, lying by the road.

A short time later, step, step, step,
someone came down the road.
It was a man who worked in God's temple.
He could help the hurt man!
But, no, when he saw the hurt man,
he crossed the road.
He passed by on the other side!
Soon another man came.
But he passed by, too.

Then, clop, clop, clip, clop,
along came a man on a donkey.
This was a man from a different country.
When he saw the hurt man, he stopped.
He put bandages on his hurt places.
And he took the man to a house
where he could rest and get well.

Jesus finished his story.
He looked at the man.
"Who was a neighbor to the hurt man?"
Jesus asked.
"The one who helped him," said the man.
"Then you can be a neighbor to anyone
who needs your help," said Jesus.

Listening

Once there were two sisters.

One was named Mary.

One was named Martha.

Jesus was their good friend.

He came to see them whenever he was in town.

MARY & MARTHA, from Luke 10

One time while Jesus was at their house,
he had a long talk with Mary.
Mary sat by Jesus.
She listened and listened.
Jesus had so many wonderful things to say.

Martha was thinking about other things.
She knew there was a lot of work to do.
She wanted to get their dinner ready.
She wanted to clean the house.
She wanted to make a nice bed for Jesus.
And while Martha worked, worked, worked,
Mary sat and listened.

Finally Martha got upset.

"Jesus," she said, "Mary is not helping.

I am doing all this work by myself.

Tell her to come and help me!"

"Martha, Martha," Jesus said.
"You are upset about so many things.
Mary is doing something very important.
She is listening to me.
She chose to do the best thing."

The Woman Who Could Not Stand Up

Saturdays were special days for God's people.
They called Saturday the Sabbath.
God had said it was a day for resting.
And it was a day the people worshipped God.
Some of the leaders of God's people
made up rules for the Sabbath.
"There are six days for work," they said.
"You must not do *any* work on the Sabbath."

One Sabbath, Jesus was teaching the people.
A crippled woman was there.
She was bent over.
She could not stand up straight.

When Jesus saw her, he told her
to come to him.
Then he said to her, "You are now made well."
He put his hands on her.
Right away she stood straight and tall.
And she praised God.

The leaders were angry.
They said, "Jesus, you worked when you
made this woman well.
You worked on the Sabbath day!"

But Jesus said, "You take your donkey
and your ox to get water on the Sabbath day.
That is work, too.
If you can do that kind of work,
then I can heal this woman."
They knew Jesus was right.
And all the people were excited about
the wonderful things Jesus was doing.

411

The Lost Sheep

Jesus liked to tell stories
that had special meanings.
One time he told this story.

"Pretend you are a shepherd," Jesus said.
"You have 100 sheep.
You take good care of them.
You show them where the sweetest grass is.
You show them where the coolest water is.
You know each one of your sheep.
And you love them all.

Every night as you take them to their pen,
you count your sheep.
You want to be sure they are all there,
safe and sound.
When you count '100,'
you know they are all there.
You close the gate and the sheep sleep safely.

But one night, you are counting . . .

95, 96, 97, 98, 99 . . . 99?

Only 99 sheep?

You count again, but there are only 99 sheep.

The other sheep must be lost!

Do you say, 'Oh well, at least I have 99 sheep?'

No, you go to find that lost sheep.

You look and look and look.
and when at last you find it,
you carry it home on your shoulders.
You are so happy that you call your friends.
'Look,' you say, 'I found my lost sheep!'"

Then Jesus told the special meaning
of this story.
"God is like the shepherd," he said.
"God loves his people.
If one of them disobeys him,
he's like the lost sheep.
But when he is sorry and comes back to God,
God is happy.
God is like a shepherd who has found
his lost sheep!"

The Lost Coin

"Once there was a woman who had
ten silver coins," said Jesus.
"Sometimes she would count them.
One, two, three, four, five, six,
seven, eight, nine, ten . . . ten coins.
One day something was wrong.
One, two, three, four, five, six,
seven, eight, nine . . . nine?
Only nine?
Where could the other coin be?

She lit her lamp so she could see
under the furniture.
She even swept her house looking for the coin.
Suddenly she saw it!
She picked it up and called her friends.
'Be happy with me,' she said.
'I have found my lost coin.'"

God is like that woman.
He wants to find his people
who are not following him.
They are lost from him.
He wants them to follow him again.
Then they will be found,
and God will be happy!

The Lost Son

"There was once a man who had two sons,"
said Jesus.
"The younger son was not happy at home.
He dreamed of an exciting life far away.
One day, he decided to leave his home.
So he went to his dad.
'I know that part of your land is mine,'
he said.
'I want you to pay me for my share.'

423

The father gave the son what he wanted.

The son took it all and went far away.

At first he was happy.

He did whatever he wanted to do.

He went wherever he wanted to go.

He bought whatever he wanted to buy.

Before long he spent all his money.

He did not even have the money to buy food.

So he got a job feeding pigs.

He was sad.

He wanted to go home.

He was also afraid.

Maybe his father would not like him anymore.

But he began the long trip home.

At least he could be a servant instead of a son.

His father saw him coming.
He ran to meet him.
He hugged and kissed him.
'Let's have a party,' he said.
'My son was lost, but now he is found!'"
God is like this father.
He is full of joy when someone decides
to obey him.

The Man Who Remembered

Ten men were very sad.
They were sad, because they were sick.
They were so sick, they had to
live away from their families.
They had to live away from their friends.

One day the ten men found out
that Jesus was coming their way.
They decided to go meet him.
When they saw him, they called, "Jesus, Jesus!"
Jesus looked.
And he said, "Go to the priest.
Let him take a look at you."

Now the priest was the one
who could tell them if they were well.
He could tell them if they could
live with their families again.
So they started on their way to see the priest.

While the men were walking,
they began to notice something.
They were feeling better.
They were looking better.
In fact, they were all well!

They were so excited.
They hurried on to see the priest.
All but one.
One man remembered something.
He remembered to go back to Jesus
and say thank you.

The Children

Mothers held their babies as they walked.
Boys and girls skipped and hopped
down the road.
They were happy.
They were going to see Jesus.

But when they got to the place
where Jesus was, Jesus' friends told them
to go away.
"You cannot come to see Jesus," they said.
"He is too busy for children.
He has important things to do."

Now Jesus found out
what his friends were saying.
He was angry.
"Do not stop the children," he said.
"Let them come to me."

So they came:
little boys and little girls,
and even babies.
They came to Jesus.
And Jesus took them in his arms.

He was not too busy.

He held them.

He blessed them.

He loved them.

Children are important to Jesus.

The Blind Beggar

His name was Bartimaeus.
And he could not see.
He could not work like other men did
to get money to buy food.
So every day, he sat beside the road.
He asked the people who passed by
to give him money.

BARTIMAEUS, from Mark 10

One day he heard a lot of people passing by.
"There are so many people," he said.
"What's going on?"
"Jesus is coming," they told him.

Right away Bartimaeus began calling, "Jesus!"
The people turned to Bartimaeus.
"Shhhh!" they said. "Be quiet!"
But he shouted even louder, "Jesus! Jesus!"

Jesus heard Bartimaeus.

He stopped.

"What do you want me to do for you?" he asked.

"Oh, Jesus," said Bartimaeus.

"Please make my eyes see!"

Then Jesus said, "Your eyes may see,
because you believed."
All of a sudden, Bartimaeus could see!
He could see all the colors and shapes.
He could see all the people.
He could see Jesus.
He praised God.
All the people praised God, too.

A Small Man

Zacchaeus was a man who took tax money
from people.
Tax money was what they had to pay
to their king.
But Zacchaeus took more money
than he was supposed to.
He kept it to make himself rich.
And nobody liked him.

One day, Jesus was passing by his town.

Everyone went to see Jesus.

Even Zacchaeus went to see Jesus.

But Zacchaeus had a problem.

He was short.

Everyone was in his way.

He could not see.

Then Zacchaeus had an idea.
He ran ahead of all the people.
He climbed a tall tree.
He had found the perfect place to watch Jesus.
He could see all the people coming.

When Jesus got to the tree, he stopped.
He looked up at Zacchaeus.
"Zacchaeus," he said, "come down right away.
I need to stay at your house today!"

Zacchaeus scrambled down that tree.
Jesus wanted to stay with him!
He took Jesus to his house.
He told Jesus, "I want to do what is right.
I will give back the money I took
to make me rich."
Jesus was pleased.
Zacchaeus had chosen to do the right thing.

Two Small Coins

The temple was big and beautiful.
Many people came there to worship God.
Inside the temple were some big money boxes.
They were open at the top,
so the people could put money in them.
The money was for the temple
and all that was used in worship to God.

One day Jesus sat down across from
the money boxes.
He saw many rich people put in lots of money.
Then one poor woman walked up to the boxes.
She put in two small coins.

Jesus looked at his friends.
"This poor woman put in more
than the rich people did," he said.
"Here's why: the rich people
still have much money left.
But this woman only had two coins.
She did not have any more money.
The rich people only gave part
of what they had.
She gave all of what she had."

The Man at the Pool

There was once a very special pool.
The water was calm most of the time.
But sometimes it bubbled and bubbled.
Sick people came to this pool.
When the water bubbled,
they got into the pool.
Then they would feel well.

One day Jesus was walking by the pool.
There he saw a man who could not walk.
The man had been lame for a long time.
So Jesus asked the man,
"Do you want to get well?"

"Oh, yes, I do," said the man.
"But I do not know anyone who will help me
get into the pool when the water bubbles."
Then Jesus said, "Get up.
Pick up your mat and walk."

Right away the man's legs were well.
He stood up and he walked!
The leaders of the people were angry,
because it was the Sabbath day.
They thought the man should not carry
his mat on the Sabbath.
But Jesus said, "God is always working,
even today.
So I am working, too."

Mary's Gift

Mary and Martha were two
of Jesus' good friends.
They were getting ready
for a big dinner party at their house.
It was a dinner for Jesus.
They had invited all his good friends.

That night many people sat down
together at Mary and Martha's table.
Martha was busy as always.
She carried the food to the table.

But Mary did a surprising thing.
She took some perfume that cost
a lot of money.
She poured it on Jesus' feet.
Then she wiped his feet with her hair.
Mmmm! It made the whole house smell sweet!

One of Jesus' friends was named Judas.
He said, "Why didn't Mary sell this perfume?
She could give us the money.
Then we could give it to the poor people."
But Judas said this because *he* really
wanted the money.
He was the keeper of the money bag.
He took money out of the bag
when no one was looking.
He spent the money on himself.

"Leave Mary alone," said Jesus.
"She gave this perfume to me as a gift,
because I will not always be able
to be here with you."

Make Way for the King

Two of Jesus' friends went
to look for a donkey.
Jesus had told them just where to find it.
It would be tied right by the village gate.
It was going to be a special donkey.
Jesus was going to ride on it.

TRIUMPHAL ENTRY, from John 12

When the friends found the donkey,
they took it to Jesus.
They put their coats on its back,
and Jesus got on.

When the people saw Jesus coming,
they began to shout with joy.
"Hosanna! Hosanna!
Blessed is the King who comes
in the name of the Lord!"

Some people cut branches off the palm trees.
They laid the branches on the road.
Other people spread their coats on the road.
And they all praised God in loud voices
for the wonderful things Jesus had done.

Jesus rode to the big city of Jerusalem.
The crowds followed him.
The leaders of the people were angry.
"See how all the people follow Jesus now?
They do not follow us anymore.
We must get rid of Jesus," they said.

Washing Feet

Jesus knew that not everyone liked him.
He knew the leaders were angry with him.
In fact, they were so angry and so jealous,
they wanted to kill him.
And Jesus knew that, too.

But Jesus still had his special friends:
Peter, Andrew, James, John, Philip,
Bartholomew, Simon, Matthew, James,
Thomas, Thaddaeus and Judas.
They had been his friends for a long time.
They traveled with Jesus.
And Jesus taught them many things.

One night, they all got together for dinner.
While they were eating, Jesus got up.
He put a towel on like an apron.
He poured water into a large bowl.
Then he began to wash his friends' feet.

When Jesus got to Peter's feet,
Peter said, "I cannot let you wash my feet."
"If you don't let me wash your feet,
you can't follow me," said Jesus.
"In that case," said Peter, "wash my hands
and my head, too!"

After Jesus washed his friends' feet,
he asked, "Do you understand what I did?
I showed you how to be kind to each other.
I am your Lord and Teacher.
If I can be kind and help you,
then you can be kind and help each other."

The Last Supper

Judas, one of Jesus' friends, had a bad idea.
He knew that the leaders were angry with Jesus.
He knew they wanted to catch Jesus
Now Judas wanted money more than anything.
So he told the leaders that he would
show them where Jesus was if they would
pay him some money.
They paid him 30 pieces of silver.

IN THE UPPER ROOM, from Matthew 26

One night, Jesus and his friends
were eating supper together.
"One of you is planning to do something
bad to me," Jesus said.
"Who is it?" asked John.

Jesus said, "It is the one I give bread to."
Then he gave a piece of bread to Judas.
"Go on," Jesus told him.
"Do what you are planning to do."
Judas got up and left.
Only Judas and Jesus knew
what Judas' bad idea was.

Then Jesus gave thanks, and broke some bread.
He shared it with his friends.
Next he took a cup of wine and gave thanks.
He shared this with his friends, too.
"Whenever you eat the bread and drink
the wine, remember me," he said.

Then Jesus said, "I will not be
with you much longer.
I have to leave.
But do not worry.
Do not be afraid.
I will come back.
You are my friends.
Love each other as I love you."

Sadness

It was night.
Jesus took his friends to a garden.
There Jesus prayed.
And there Judas carried out his bad idea.
He led soldiers to the garden.
He showed them where Jesus was.
Jesus knew he would.
And it was all right.
Jesus went with them.

THE CRUCIFIXION, from John 18 & 19

You see, it was time for Jesus to die.
God had planned it long ago.
Jesus knew it would happen
when he came to the earth.
He came to take the punishment
for all the wrong things anybody
had ever done, or ever would do.
And now it was time.
The soldiers took him to the leaders.

The leaders did not believe he was God's Son.
They said, "He must die, because
he calls himself the Son of God."
So they killed him on a cross.
It was a sad day for Jesus' friends.
But they did not know that God had planned
a wonderful surprise for them.
And they would not be sad for long!

Surprise!

After Jesus died, a rich man named Joseph
took Jesus' body.
He put it in a special cave-tomb.
He rolled a huge stone
over the opening of the cave.
The leaders sent guards to watch the cave
to make sure no one took Jesus' body.

But early Sunday morning,
there was an earthquake.
An angel came from heaven
and rolled the stone away.
When the guards saw him,
they shook with fear and fell down.

One of Jesus' friends named Mary
came to the cave-tomb early that morning.
She saw the stone was not in front of it,
so she went in.
She saw an angel there.
"Jesus is not here," the angel said.
"He is alive!
Go tell his friends that they will get to
see him again!"

Mary was not sad anymore.

Jesus was not dead.

He was alive!

She ran back to tell the wonderful news.

At first, Jesus' friends did not believe her.

But she was right!

Jesus did come back to see them.

He really *was* alive!

Fish for Breakfast

Late one day, Peter, James and John,
and some of Jesus' other friends
were together by the Sea of Galilee.
"I'm going fishing," said Peter.
"We will go with you," said the others.

WITH THE RISEN JESUS, from John 21

They sailed out in their boat.
They threw their net into the water.
And they waited and waited and waited.
All night they fished,
but they did not catch anything.

Early in the morning, they saw someone
standing on the shore.
He called, "Have you caught any fish?"
"No," they yelled.
"Throw your net on the other side
of the boat," the man called.
So they threw the net on the other side.

All at once, fish filled the net.
John looked at Peter.
"It's Jesus!" he said.
Peter was so excited,
he jumped into the water.
He swam to the shore.

It *was* Jesus!

He made a little campfire.

He cooked fish and bread on it.

"Come and have some breakfast," Jesus called.

They did not have to ask who he was.

They knew he was their best friend Jesus.

He was alive!

Jesus Goes Home

Jesus led his friends to a place near Bethany.
He lifted his hands up and blessed them.
"Tell other people about me," he said.
Then he went up into the sky.
A cloud hid him,
so his friends could not see him.
They stood looking up into the sky
for a long time.

JESUS ASCENDS INTO HEAVEN, from Matthew 28 & Acts 1

All of a sudden, two angels stood beside them.
"Why are you still looking into the sky?"
the angels asked.
"Jesus has gone up to heaven.
Someday he will come back
the same way you saw him leave."
Then the friends went back to the city
with joy in their hearts.

Jesus had taught them many things.
They would always remember that he said,
"Do not worry or be afraid.
Trust in God and trust in me.
In God's house there are many rooms.
I will go to make a place ready for you.
Someday I will come back and take you
with me so you can be where I am."

Wind and Fire

Before Jesus went home to be with God,
he told his friends to stay in Jerusalem.
He said they would get a gift there.
So they waited in Jerusalem.

THE DAY OF PENTECOST, from Acts 2

Now there was a great holiday coming
called Pentecost.
Many people came to Jerusalem
from far and near to celebrate that day.
The friends of Jesus celebrated, too.

Suddenly they heard a sound
like a strong wind blowing.
And they saw something that looked like
little flames of fire resting on them.
Then God's Holy Spirit filled them.
This was the gift Jesus had told them
to wait for!

They began to speak in languages
they did not know.
The people who were there from other
countries heard Jesus' friends speaking.
And they could understand them.
The languages Jesus' friends were speaking
were the same languages they spoke.
The people were amazed!

"This is what God promised us," Peter said.
Then he told them about Jesus.
Many people believed in Jesus that day.

Peter and John and the Beggar

There once was a man who could not walk.
Every day he sat at the gate to the temple.
He begged people to give him some money
so he could buy food and clothes.

HEALED IN JESUS' NAME, from Acts 3

One afternoon, Peter and John went
to the temple.
The beggar man saw them.
He asked them for some money.
When Peter and John looked at him,
he thought they were going to give him money.

"We do not have any silver or gold,"
said Peter.
"But we will be glad to give you
what we have.
In the name of Jesus, walk."
Peter took the man by the hand
and helped him up.

Right away, the man's feet grew strong.
He walked.
He jumped.
He went into the temple praising God.

When the people saw him, they were amazed.
"It is Jesus' power
that has made this man well," said Peter.
Then all the people began to praise God,
because the lame man could walk.

A Bright Light

There was once a very mean man named Saul.
He did not like anyone who loved Jesus.
He wanted to catch them and put them in jail.
He traveled near and far to find them.
One of his trips took him
to the big city of Damascus.

SAUL IS CONVERTED, from Acts 9

While he was on his way,
a bright light suddenly flashed from the sky.
It shone all around Saul.
Saul closed his eyes.
A voice called, "Saul, Saul,
why are you doing these mean things?"
Saul was scared!

"Who are you?" Saul asked.

"I am Jesus," said the voice.

"Now get up and go to the city.

There you will find out what to do."

Saul got up.

But when he opened his eyes, he could not see.

His friends had to lead him to the city.

In that city lived a good man named Ananias.
Jesus came to him in a dream and said,
"Go find Saul."
So Ananias went to Saul.
He touched Saul and said,
"Jesus sent me so you could see again.
Jesus wants you to be one of his friends."

Right away, Saul could see again.
He got up and was baptized.
And he was not mean anymore.
He even changed his name.
Now everyone called him Paul.
And for the rest of his life,
Paul told others about Jesus.

Paul and Silas in Jail

Paul had a very good friend named Silas.
They went near and far telling about Jesus.
Many people believed
and became followers of Jesus.
They were called Christians.
But some people did not believe.
They did not like Christians.

A JAILER BELIEVES, from Acts 16

In one town, these men
put Paul and Silas in jail.
But Paul and Silas did not worry.
They knew God was with them everywhere.
Even in jail!
They sang and prayed in jail.

The other people in jail listened.
About midnight, there was an earthquake.
The chains on the prisoners fell off!
All the jail doors flew open!
The jailer woke up and ran into the jail.
He was afraid everyone had run away.

But Paul and Silas called, "We are all here."
The jailer could hardly believe it.
He asked Paul and Silas what to do.
"Believe in Jesus," they told him.
And he did believe.
He let Paul and Silas out of jail.
Then he and his family were baptized.
And their hearts were full of joy and love.

The Door into Heaven

John was one of Jesus' best friends.

He told many people about Jesus.

People began to follow Jesus' way.

The leaders did not like this.

They sent John away to an island

so he could not tell anyone about Jesus.

Onc day John heard a voice behind him.
It was loud like a trumpet.
John turned around.
He saw Jesus, shining like the sun.
"Do not be afraid," said Jesus.
"Write about what you see."

Then John saw an open door in heaven.
He saw God's throne
with a rainbow around it.
All day and night, creatures with wings kept
saying, "Holy, holy, holy is the Lord God
Almighty, who was and is and is to come."
John saw what was going to happen.
He saw the devil and his helpers
being thrown into a lake of fire.

525

He saw a new Heaven and a new earth.
He saw a new city of God.
A loud voice said, "God's people
will live with God now.
They will not need the sun or moon.
God's glory will give them light.
There will be no more dying
or crying or hurting.
God's people will live with Him
for ever and ever."
Then Jesus said, "I am coming soon."
And John said, "YES, JESUS, COME."

To discover more great reading for children…

(turn this page!)

THE BEGINNER'S DEVOTIONAL

s-10 • 384 pages • text by Stephen T. Barclift • illustrations by Jerry Werner

⌐R DEVOTIONS KIDS LOVE, this is the book to explore! Arranged by seasons of the year and enhanced with 250 full-color pictures, THE BEGINNER'S DEVOTIONAL includes 52 devotions, each of which can be done all in one sitting, or broken down into six different parts to complete at various times through the week.

Each devotion includes:
- a story for today (each one revolving around the life of the Kenton family and their three growing, fun-loving children);
- an introduction to a story from the Bible (with optional cross-references to Bible stories in both *THE EARLY READER'S BIBLE* and *THE BEGINNER'S BIBLE);*
- a list of questions about the story;
- a Scripture memory verse;
- suggested prayer guidelines;
- and a fun family activity.

A complete topical index directs parents to quick help on character development issues (great for family problem-solving and encouragement!).

This is the book to enhance any child's desire to grow in the Lord!

WHAT WOULD JESUS DO?
The Classic Novel IN HIS STEPS...Now Retold for Children

For ages 3-10 • 256 pages • text by Mack Thomas • illustrations by Denis Mortenson
tape cassette produced by Tony Salerno

AS BOTH a book and audio cassette, *WHAT WOULD JESUS DO?* presents the stirring call to follow Christ in a way young children can easily understand and embrace.

The delightful book text is written in short, simple sentences, and set in a clear typeface especially recommended for early readers. Each short chapter focuses in a fresh way on the book's core concept—learning to ask throughout the day, *What would Jesus do?*

Discussion questions for each chapter help parents and teachers highlight this truth for children. And enhancing the text are full-color illustrations on more than two hundred pages.

The tape cassette includes the complete book text recorded with professional character voices, and with a stirring music background.

By creatively imparting the call of Christ in the years when children are so impressionable, *WHAT WOULD JESUS DO?* is a story to truly change the course of future generations!